Are You Ready for the Rapture?

Don't Be Left Behind When Jesus Comes Again

Barbara Lockhart

Contents

Introduction

The Rapture is...

The rapture is the event foretold in the Bible where Christian Believers—both dead and alive— are caught up to meet Jesus in the air.

❖

For the Lord himself will come down from heaven with a commanding shout, with the voice of the archangel, and with the trumpet call of God. First, the believers who have died will rise from their graves. Then, together with them, we who are still alive and remain on the earth will be caught up in the clouds to meet the Lord in the air. Then we will be with the Lord forever.

(I Thessalonians 4:16-17 New Living Translation)

Chapter 1

Prepared, Not Scared

On Thanksgiving Day 1939, my two older and two younger brothers, along with my little sister and two other children Mamma cared for, thought the rapture had certainly happened. Since 4:30 that afternoon, all of us had taken turns pressing our faces against the foggy window of our little farm house in search of our pastor's shiny, new Hudson coming down the dusty dirt road to pick us up.

That morning when Pastor came to take Mamma to the rental hall so she could cook the Thanksgiving dinner for our growing church family, he promised to come back for us in plenty of time to enjoy the lavish turkey dinner. We waited all day, careful not to eat, so we'd have lots of room for the feast. The excitement of riding in Pastor's new car began to wear off as darkness fell. Now all our faces were pressed against the window hoping to see headlights coming our way. There were no cell phones—we didn't have a phone, period, nor a car, not even a bicycle. We didn't focus on what we didn't have, however, but were thankful we had a home, a church, and parents who worked hard to keep food on the table.

"Do you think Pastor has forgotten us?" I asked timidly.

"Oh no!" Teddy, the oldest, responded. "A pastor always does what he says." Teddy's voice trailed off as he thought about what other possibilities might be the reason for Pastor's delay. Suddenly, he panicked. Teddy screamed, "It's the rapture! The rapture happened! Mama and Pastor have gone to heaven."

Instantly, everyone was crying—even the two year olds; although, they didn't know why. There was a lot of repenting going on and asking Jesus to forgive us when Pastor finally arrived. He had indeed forgotten us, so by the time we got to the dining hall, there was no food left. We were hungry, but thankful we hadn't missed the most important event in human history since the resurrection and ascension of Jesus over 2,000 years ago.

In 1939, as children, we didn't understand the prophecies in the Bible that would be fulfilled prior to the rapture. Today, however, we who call ourselves Christians, regardless of our denominational labels, have no excuse not to study the Scriptures.

Ancient Prophecies Coming to Pass

Daily, the news media around the world is a reminder of what the prophets Isaiah, Zechariah, Daniel, Joel, and even Jesus predicted would happen preceding the rapture. Jesus said:

When you see the events I've described beginning to happen, you can know His return is very near, right at the door.

Matthew 24:33

Followed by this specific confirmation:

I assure you this generation will not pass from the scene before all these things take place.

verse 34

Jesus goes on to explain:

When the Son of man returns, it will be like it was in Noah's day. In these days before the flood the people were enjoying banquets and parties and weddings right up to the time Noah entered his boat. People didn't realize what was going to happen until the Flood came and swept them all away. That is the way it will be when the Son of Man comes.

verses 37-41

Jesus continues with this scenario:

Two men will be working in the field. One will be taken, the other left. Two women will be grinding flour at the mill. One will be taken, the other left.

Matthew 24:40

And then this admonition:

SO BE PREPARED because you don't know what day your Lord will be coming.

Matthew 24:42

Wouldn't we be wise to be ready for the greatest event in the history of the modern church? After the rapture, it will be too late to miss all the destruction, plagues, and Battle of Armageddon. Wouldn't you rather be one of those returning with Jesus?

If you are reading this booklet before the rapture, you can still get ready to be taken and not be left behind. As Jesus said:

Take note. I will come as unexpectedly as a thief! Blessed are all who are watching for me who keep their robes ready so they will not need to walk naked and ashamed.

Revelation 16:15

Let us not fear; but rather, let us learn what it takes to get approved to meet Jesus in the air. That way, we can pray in confidence, "Come, Lord Jesus." (Revelation 22:25)

The Apostle Paul wrote this to the new Christian church:

We believe that Jesus died and rose again and so we believe that God will bring with Jesus those who have fallen asleep in him. According to the Lord's own word, we tell you that we who are still alive, who are left till the coming of the Lord, will certainly not precede those who have fallen asleep. For the Lord himself will come down from heaven, with a loud command, with the voice of the archangel and with the trumpet call of God, and the dead in Christ will rise first. After that, we who are still alive and are left will be caught up together with them in the clouds to meet the Lord in the air. And so we will be with the Lord forever. Therefore encourage each other with these words.

I Thessalonians 4:14-18

Prayerfully Consider

How do you feel about meeting Jesus? Are you confident in your love for and from the Lord?

Such love has no fear, because perfect love expels all fear. If we are afraid, it is for fear of punishment, and this shows that we have not fully experienced his perfect love.

I John 4:18

Chapter 2

The Spirit and the Bride Say, "Come"

Revelation 22:17

*You must love the Lord your God with all your **heart**, all your **soul**, and all your **strength**.*

Deuteronomy 6:5

How much do you love God? How do you measure your love for God?

Recently, my husband and I attended a memorial service for a teenager who was tragically killed in an automobile accident. Her parents, along with their other six children, expressed their love for her. Her father relayed this story:

"When my daughter was small, she and I would play a game. She held her hands about 12 inches apart, and with a twinkle in her eye, she said, 'Daddy, I love you this much.' I'd respond by holding my arms wide open and say, 'I love you this much.' Then she'd say, 'I love you from here to the wall.' I'd say, 'I love you all around the house.' Then she'd say, 'Well, I love you clear around the world.'"

God's very first commandment states we are to love Him with all our hearts. The heart implies we are to have an emotional connection to God. When you think about your relationship with God, do you get emotional about Him?

A Test of Love

The Apostle Peter loved Jesus, but when his love was tested, he wasn't so sure. Shortly after the Lord's Supper, Peter said, "Lord, I am ready to go to prison with you, and even die with you." (Luke 22:33)

But Jesus said, "Peter, let me tell you something. The rooster will not crow tomorrow morning until you have denied me three times."

Sure enough, Luke 22:54-62 recites the three times Peter denied the Lord.

Later when Peter heard the rooster crow, he left the courtyard where he had followed Jesus *afar off* after Jesus was arrested and *cried bitterly*.

What is your attitude about your relationship with Jesus? Do all your friends, family, and associates know you love the Lord and that He is first in your life? Or, are you like the man who said to his wife, "Nobody in the sales meeting today could tell I'm a Christian"?

Have you ever been around a young lady who just got engaged? She's showing off her ring and telling anyone who will listen how much she's in love and how wonderful her husband-to-be is. How often do you tell Jesus how much you love Him?

Prayerfully Consider

Do you get excited when you have a chance to tell someone about the Lord, or are you one of those who says, "My religion is a private matter. I don't talk about it"?

You are the light of the world—like a city on a mountain, glowing in the night for all to see. Don't hide your light under a basket! Instead, put it on a stand and let it shine for all.

Matthew 5:14-15

If you want to grow in your love for the Lord, answer the Holy Spirit's call, "Come."

Come, let us spend time communicating with our Lord in prayer and getting to know Him better through His Word. The more we know Him, the more we grow to love Him.

Chapter 3

Self-Sacrificing Love

Jesus, after His resurrection, asked Peter, "Do you love me more than these?"

In the Greek language, there is more than one word for *love*. The word Jesus used here for *love* is *agape*, which means "sacrificial love." It is the same Greek word for love used in John 3:16: "For God so loved the world."

Peter knew he had, just a few days prior, denied Jesus. How could he say yes when his actions had recently proven that he didn't have the self-sacrificial, *agape* love for Jesus yet?

Feeling stuck, Peter answered, "Lord, you know I *phileo* love you." (*Phileo* is the Greek word for "brotherly love.") He could honestly say he had brotherly love for Jesus.

When Jesus asked Peter for the third time if he loved Him, Jesus used the Greek word *phileo* instead of *agape*. (John 21:17) Peter was grieved! Now Jesus had down-graded the level of love in His inquiry. Peter's response was, "Lord, you know all things; you know that I have *phileo* (brotherly love) for you."

Power from Heaven

Later, Jesus let Peter know as he continued to follow Him, he would sacrifice his life for the gospel (verse 18).

When the Day of Pentecost came and Peter was filled with the Holy Spirit, he had new boldness and power. He proved that he had *agape* love for his Savior.

Peter stood up in front of an international crowd—some who had heard him deny his association with Jesus before the crucifixion. But now, instead of cowering in fear, Peter preached boldly, telling the listeners that Jesus was the Lord and that they needed to repent and be baptized.

Following the lives of Peter and the other apostles, we read in Acts 4-5 that they were threatened, beaten, and thrown in prison for their faith. Yet, they continued to speak out for Jesus. Their faith was unstoppable!

Peter boldly declared, "We ought to obey God rather than human authority." (Acts 5:29)

As Peter went about his ministry, the power of the Holy Spirit in him was so mighty that people brought those who were sick out into the streets on beds and mats so that when Peter walked by, his shadow fell on them and they were healed and made well! (Acts 5:15-16)

Loving Christ More than Life

Do you recall the Columbine High School shooting in Colorado on April 8, 1999, when Rachel Scott so bravely answered "yes" when the shooter asked, "Are you a Christian?"

If that had been you, how would you answer? It's a tough question, and yet one a 17-year old had to face.

Safe in our homes, it's easy for us to declare, "Yes, Lord, I'll die for you." But the next question is, will we live for Him? That is a question we do face on a daily basis.

Serving Others

Just as babies are all about getting their needs met, when we first accept Jesus as our Lord and Savior, everything is all about us. We are excited that our sins are forgiven, that we have peace, joy and hope. We are focused on our new life with all the blessings and provisions of heaven that come with it. And rightly so! But as our relationship with the Lord matures, our viewpoint should shift from asking for our own needs to caring about how we can serve God by serving others.

Let's go back to Jesus asking Peter, "Do you love me?"

After Peter answered, "Yes, Lord; you know that I love you," Jesus said to him, "Feed my sheep." What did Jesus mean by that? Jesus was directing Peter to reach out to others and take care of them. The day came when Peter defended the practice of including Gentiles (non-Jews) into the church, saying that God gave them the same gift of the Holy Spirit that they themselves had received. Thus, he ministered to all people without prejudice.

Prayerfully Consider

In what ways can you share the love of Jesus with those you come in contact with?

Let your light so shine before men that they may see your good works and glorify your Father in heaven. Matthew 5:16

Chapter 4

A Heavenly Love Story

The Song of Solomon in the Old Testament is a beautiful description of how the love relationship develops between the church (portrayed as the bride) and Jesus (portrayed as the bridegroom).

Abishag, a country girl from the land of Shuman, had worked hard all her life taking care of other people's vineyards. As a servant girl with few options for a better future, Abishag was delighted at being chosen to marry the king. At the beginning of this love story, Abishag is not ready for her royal calling. She needs time to adapt from being a slave to becoming a princess. She complains that her complexion is sun-browned and her skin calloused—the appearance of one who has been working in the sun, not living in the palace. When we first come to Christ, we may also feel like we're not worthy of our King. We've been forgiven and are clean on the inside, but there may be things about our outward life that need to be purified.

Abishag asked, "Where do you feed your flocks?" (Song of Solomon 1:7) She knows if she can watch him work, she will learn how to do what he does. Thus, she will be more prepared to share life with Solomon.

His response is, "Follow the footsteps of the flock."

Solomon also knew if Abishag learned where the sheep were feeding beside the shepherd's tents, she would learn how to take care of his kingdom.

Have you found a church where the Kingdom of God is portrayed? Have you found a place where the Spirit of God is moving? Where the Word of God is taught? Nothing helps us to grow faster than receiving good Bible teaching and experiencing God's Spirit moving in and through His people. So if you don't already attend a church that is alive with the moving of the Holy Spirit, I encourage you to seek one out.

As we continue the love story into the second chapter, Solomon is standing behind a wall looking through a latticed window at Abishag. It is now time for her to come with him. He encourages her by saying, "Rise up my fair one and come away." One of the signs of the time is the fig tree. In several places throughout Scripture, the fig tree is used symbolically.

For example, Jesus used the fig tree as a sign of the time when His return would be near.

Now learn a parable from the fig tree: when its branch has already become tender and puts forth leaves; you know summer is near. So you also, when you see all these things know that He is near—at the door!

Matthew 24:32-34

In Song of Solomon 3, night comes and Abishag misses her beloved. She runs into the streets and squares of the city looking for him.

Do you sometimes feel like you are searching everywhere and in every way trying to find the Lord? I trust that you will always remember that even in your darkest hour, Jesus can be found, just as Abishag found her bridegroom. She declared, "When I found the one I love, I held him and would not let him go." (SS 3:4) Likewise, let us hold on to Jesus and not let go of our faith nor our love for Him, especially as our world gets farther and farther from the light of the gospel.

Next, let's look at the turn of events in Song of Solomon 5. After being in his garden, Solomon goes to Abishag's door, knocks, and calls for her to come. But alas, she is too sleepy to take the trouble to get ready and open the door.

By the time Abishag finally arises and unlocks the door, she can smell the scent of Solomon, but he has gone. Her beloved has left!

Have you ever said, "I'm just too tired to go to church; I think I'll hang out and rest for a while"? I know there were times when I felt too tired; and yet, when I went anyway, I found that the Holy Spirit showed up, and people were touched and healed. I would not have wanted to miss that for anything! The problem is that we can't "rewind" a church service or a move of God. Once we've missed it, that time has passed, and it is too late for us to be there. I am not saying that there aren't valid reasons to miss a church service. I am saying that we don't want to let a weak excuse cause us to miss out when the Holy Spirit is calling. The love story of Solomon and Abishag is in the Bible for us to learn an important lesson.

Prayerfully Consider

How do you respond when the Lord comes knocking on your heart's door? To everyone who answers, the Lord will come in.

Behold, I stand at the door and knock. If anyone hears my voice and opens the door, I will come into him and dine with him and he with me.

Revelation 3:20

Chapter 5

Five Wise and Five Foolish Believers

While Jesus sat on the slopes of the Mount of Olives, His disciples came to him privately to ask about the future. Jesus foretold what would happen. (Matthew 24) And then Jesus did something that was common for their culture: He told them a parable. (Matthew 25:1-13)

Jesus began the narrative by saying:

Then the kingdom of heaven shall be likened to 10 virgins who took their lamps and went out to meet the bridegroom.

Notice first that all 10 women in the story were virgins. This showed that they were all Christ-followers who had not defiled themselves with other lovers. Second, they all took lamps, meaning they all had the light of the Word of God. The disciples were familiar with the Old Testament and understood what Jesus was saying.

Your Word is a lamp unto my feet and a light unto my path.

Psalm 119:105

Third, they were all expecting to marry the bridegroom. All of this sounds perfect, but then Jesus put a twist in the story when He said, "Now five were wise and five were foolish."

Not one, not two, not a minority—but half were foolish!

How so?

"Those who were foolish took their lamps but took no oil with them." We know in Scripture that oil is used as a symbol of the Holy Spirit. Jesus explained, "...but the wise took oil in the vessels with their lamps."

Oil in the vessels was understood to mean the Holy Spirit within them. Previously, Jesus had said:

*He is the Holy Spirit who leads into all truth. The world cannot receive him, because it isn't looking for him and doesn't recognize him. But you know him, because He lives with you now, and later will be **in you**.*

John 14:17

As the story goes on, Jesus said the bridegroom was delayed; and as a result, all ten of the virgins fell asleep.

Just as Abishag was on her bed when Solomon came (Song of Solomon 5:2), we see that in Jesus' parable, even those who have oil in their vessels also slumber.

Today, some of God's people are spiritually fast asleep. They are unaware of all the signs pointing to the return of Jesus to take His bride. Many do not even know what the Bible teaches about Jesus' return for His people.

When, at midnight (verse 6), the cry is heard, "The Bridegroom is coming, go out to meet him," will they recognize the call?

Will you?

In the last days scoffers will say:

Where is the promise of His coming? For ever since the fathers fell asleep, all things continue as they were from the beginning.

2 Peter 3:4

Jesus said:

But watch yourselves lest your hearts be weighted down with... cares of this life and that day come upon you suddenly like a trap. For it will come upon all who dwell on the face of the whole earth.

Luke 21:34-35

The original Greek writing is translated like this:

Shake sleep therefore, and pray always that you may have strength to escape all these things that will come to pass and to stand before the Son of Man.

Luke 21:36

We are warned to shake off sleep when we are tempted to grow complacent. How sad it will be for the five foolish virgins who won't have time to get their vessels filled before the Bridegroom comes! Jesus has to tell them, "I do not know you." (Matthew 25:8-12)

Given the consequences of not having oil in our vessels, wouldn't it be wise to do whatever it takes to get and keep a supply of oil? Clearly, having the lamp (Word of God) is not enough. We need the Holy Spirit, too.

I am reminded of the forewarning Jesus told His followers about false prophets and so-called Christians who were performing impressive deeds and yet did not follow God's laws:

Not everyone who calls out to me, "Lord, Lord," shall enter the Kingdom of Heaven. Only those who actually do the will of My Father in heaven will enter. On judgment day many will say to me, "Lord! Lord! We prophesied in your name, and cast out demons in your name, and did many mighty works in your name." But I will reply, "I never knew you. Get away from me, you who break God's laws."

Matthew 7:21-23

Jesus saw right through the people who claimed to be religious and righteous but did not actually do the will of His Father in heaven. No one can fool God.

...People judge by outward appearance, but the Lord looks at the heart.

I Samuel 16:7

We are all sinners who must come to repentance, accept Jesus as Savior, and follow Him. We do not impress God with our deeds. He wants our hearts.

Prayerfully Consider

Do you long for more of the Holy Spirit in your life? Be encouraged! God's promise is for you. We'll talk about this more in the next chapter.

You will find Him if you seek Him with all your heart and with all your soul.

Deuteronomy 4:29

Chapter 6

Receive Power, Boldness, and Assurance

When the 120 followers of Jesus got their "vessels" filled with the Holy Spirit as recorded in Acts 2, it was a very significant event, to say the least. It was completely life changing!

Remember the difference it made for Peter after he was filled with the Holy Spirit? He spoke the Word with boldness and after that, even Peter's shadow caused people to be healed of illness. What power!

I'll never forget the night I was filled with the Holy Spirit. I was just 16 years old. I wanted Jesus more than anything. At the end of a church service, I cried out to Him as I hurried to the prayer room. At this time, the room had a dirt floor covered in sawdust, because it was under construction. Right there, the Spirit of the Lord swept me off my feet, and for the next four hours, I laid on that sawdust-covered floor immersed in His holy presence. The glory of the Lord was beyond mortal words. A new, heavenly language flowed through me. I continued to speak in tongues for two days because of the Holy Presence of God. My life changed. I was no longer the shy girl afraid to ever raise my hand in class.

In school on Monday following my infilling of the Holy

Spirit, when the teacher asked for a volunteer to debate the subject of creation versus evolution, my hand shot up. Everyone in class, including the teacher, was shocked. Needless to say, I won the debate–with the Holy Spirit's help. I even received a standing ovation!

Today, at the age of 85, I still have the "oil" of the Holy Spirit in my "vessel." I use my heavenly prayer language daily while praying in my home; and as a result, people are getting touched by God and healed of sickness and sorrow. I'm thankful!

If you can't point to a specific time when you first experienced being filled with the Holy Spirit, I encourage you to ask Jesus to fill you and expect the love of our Lord to come down and give you a new experience that includes getting your heavenly language, because that's how the apostles knew when someone was filled with the Holy Spirit. If it doesn't happen the first time you ask, don't be discouraged. Time spent waiting on the Lord is never time wasted. God might be leading you deeper and deeper in Him. Keep seeking the Lord and trust in God's timing.

You can also ask a pastor, minister, or spiritual mentor who has received the Holy Spirit to pray with you. Here's a biblical example:

When Paul placed his hands on them, the Holy Spirit came on them, and they spoke in tongues and prophesied.

Acts 19:6

My Heartfelt Prayer

A few years ago I told the Lord, "Jesus, I don't care how you do it, when you do it, or where you do it, but I'm asking you to put me in the right place to experience what you will do in your people to get us ready for your return."

Not long after I prayed that prayer, my husband and I moved to a region where neither of us had ever lived. Now we have discovered there are pockets of people from various churches around the world who are experiencing an outpouring of the Holy Spirit. This mighty outpouring is producing miracle healings, signs and wonders, and changed lives.

Be encouraged! God's giving of the Holy Spirit is not confined to any particular church or group. The Holy Spirit is searching for those who love the Lord God with all their heart, soul, and mind (Matthew 22:37) and who worship the Father in spirit and in truth. (John 4:23)

In addition, the giving of the Holy Spirit is not confined to a particular period of time. You did not miss out because you weren't living in the New Testament times. God promised it down through the generations.

The promise (of the Holy Spirit) is for you and your children and for all who are far off—for all whom the Lord our God will call.

Acts 2:39

Yes, this Scripture is true. Ever since the Day of Pentecost, Believers have been receiving this wonderful promise from heaven, and you can, too. If you do not receive it the first or second or third time you ask, don't be disheartened. Keep on asking and going even deeper in prayer, because God knows just the right time to bless you with His precious promise.

One night, a young woman, a friend of my daughter, was lying in bed telling the Lord how much she loved Him. After a time of praising and thanking God, she felt the most wonderful heavenly love come down, and then she heard herself speaking in a beautiful new language. From that day on, she was a changed woman. My daughter said she was happier and more at peace. I share this with you to illustrate that God can bless you with the Holy Spirit in any place you choose to commune with Him. It doesn't have to be in a church necessarily.

Prayerfully Consider

Do you want more power, boldness, and assurance in your life?

Call to me, and I will answer you, and show you great and mighty things, which you do not know."

Jeremiah 33:3 New American Standard Bible

Chapter 7

Conclusion: Love is the Key

Not long ago, my husband and I were in a class that prepared volunteers to offer encouragement and prayer to patients in a Southern California hospital. One of the assignments was to get alone in order to discover what the Lord wanted to speak to us.

I located a quiet spot overlooking Santa Monica Bay. After a time of seeking the Lord, Jesus asked me the same question He asked Peter, "Do you love me?"

After reflecting on the question and remember what Peter's response had been, I responded by saying, "Jesus, I am sure you know how I love you, but I want to love you more."

When we returned to the classroom, I stood and read my report. All was quiet, then the teacher said, "Barbara, you talk about Jesus too much. Please change your attitude about Jesus when you visit our patients here in the hospital."

Can you imagine? Here I'd been telling Jesus that I wanted to love Him more, and the head of the volunteer program wanted me to tone it down. Needless to say, we did not last very long in that hospital.

If a person is ashamed of me and my message, I, the Son of Man, will be ashamed of that person when I return in my glory and in the glory of the Father and the holy angels.

Luke 9:26

The Importance of Love

God, through the writings of the Apostle Paul, made it clear that having love is more important than having all kinds of talents and gifts, because without love, talents and gifts mean nothing.

Though I speak with the tongues of men and angels, but have not love, I have become like a sounding brass and clanging cymbal. And though I have the gift of prophecy and understand all mysteries and all knowledge and though I have all faith so that I could move mountains but have not love, I am nothing. And though I below all my goods to feed the poor and though I give my body to be burned, but have not love, it profits me nothing.

I Corinthians 13:1-4

Do you recall what Jesus said about the first church in Revelation 2:4? "Nevertheless I have this against you, that you have left your first love." The early church started out performing miracles because they were so in love with Jesus, they wanted to see Him glorified and for Him to receive His inheritance for which He died. Because of their love for Jesus, they were also hated and persecuted. We see a parallel of this in our love story in the Song of Solomon.

In Song of Solomon 5:6-10 when Abishag opened the door and found her lover was going, she ran throughout the city searching for him. The watchmen struck her and wounded her. They even took her veil from her. The other daughters in the city made fun of her. They questioned, "Why is your lover so special? Why is he better than anyone else?"

This is a picture of the churches and the Bride of Christ who is so in love with Jesus, she is searching in church after church to find someplace she can feel at liberty to express her love. Sadly, she finds the leadership—watchmen—don't want her and chase her away, wounding her. Even congregations—daughters—don't understand. They ask, "Why is Jesus so special? Why do you have to be singing love songs to Him? Why can't you be happy with our programs and social events?"

Love, not Perfection

God is not looking for a perfect person, which is a good thing, because we are all sinners saved by grace. God is looking for someone who loves Him (and turns from sin).

In Jesus' day, it was popular to be religious and to be a perfect keeper of all of the Old Testament rules and regulations. These were the Pharisees. One day, Jesus accepted an invitation from a Pharisee to enjoy a meal with him. As they were eating, a woman with a reputation for immoral behavior, approached Jesus with a beautiful jar of expensive perfume. She knelt at Jesus' feet, crying and washing His feet.

31

She dried His feet with her hair and then rubbed them with her costly perfume. The Pharisees were aghast! How dare Jesus let such a woman, a known prostitute, touch Him!

But Jesus said, "I tell you, her sins—and they are many— have been forgiven, so she has shown me much love."

Jesus was more impressed by a sinner who loved Him deeply than He was by the super-religious, self-righteous popular crowd. The account ends with Jesus saying to the woman, "Your faith has saved you; go in peace." (Luke 7:36-50)

Love and The Bachelor

A wealthy and handsome bachelor fell in love with a rather plain and very imperfect woman. In spite of her many shortcomings, he was crazy for her, so intending to broach the subject of marriage, he asked, "Darling, how do you feel about me?"

After thinking for a quick moment, she shrugged and said, "Meh."

In spite of this disappointing response, the bachelor loved her so much, he persisted in the conversation.

"My darling, would you spend more time with me so we can see where this relationship goes?"

"Sorry," she replied, "but I'm really too busy."

"What are you so busy with?" he asked.

"I've got my work, and I like to go to the gym after, then when I've got dinner done, I have my shows on television that I watch."

"And weekends?" he asked, still hopeful.

"Weekends are busy, too. It's the time when I do my chores, hang with friends, go biking, skiing or to the beach in summer. Saturday nights I go to the movies or out dancing or to a party. It's just really busy. There's always something going on."

"I see. What about Sunday? Could you set aside a couple hours on Sunday morning to spend with me?"

"I don't think so. Sunday is my day to sleep in, make an omelet or strawberry waffle, go shopping, check out garage sales, chat on Facebook. But I'll tell you what. I will see you on Easter Sunday and on Christmas Eve. How about that?" To her way of thinking, that should be enough. She really could not afford to sacrifice her time beyond a couple times a year.

"If that's all the time you have, I will take it. So may I communicate with you by letter? I've written out everything we need for a loving, successful long-term relationship," asked the bachelor. By now, his heart was truly aching, but he thought if she would read what he'd recorded on paper, he could still have a chance at winning her heart.

The woman pulled a face. "I'm not really a letter-reading type of person. When I read, it's usually the news online, or I like a good mystery," she replied.

"I understand." Although the bachelor was heartbroken, he accepted her decision. He then left the busy woman and did not bother her again.

Like the bachelor in this story, Jesus will knock on your heart's door, but if you don't care to participate in a relationship with Him, he will let you be. And when the day comes for the wedding, you will not be part of the group called the bride.

When Jesus comes to take His people out of the earth and into the great wedding feast in heaven, He is looking for those who are in love with Him. He is not looking for a bride who is indifferent. That makes sense, doesn't it?

As you prayerfully consider the Scriptures in this short book and what they mean for you, I pray that you will fall more and more in love with Jesus, so that when the time comes to meet the Lord, you are not only ready, but eager to go to the great wedding feast in heaven.

Then I heard again what sounded like the shout of a vast crowd or the roar of mighty ocean waves or the crash of loud thunder:

"Praise the Lord!

For the Lord our God, the Almighty, reigns.

Let us be glad and rejoice, and let us give honor to him.

for the time has come for the wedding feast of the Lamb, and his bride has prepared herself.

She has been given the finest of pure white linen to wear."

For the fine linen represents the good deeds of God's holy people.

And the angel said to me, "Write this: Blessed are those who are invited to the wedding feast of the Lamb." And he added, "These are true words that come from God."

Revelation 19:6-9

Dear Reader:

Thank you for taking the time to read this short work. It has been on my heart for many years to get the message out about the event we call the rapture and the great wedding feast in heaven.

This is not intended to be a scholarly work; but rather, a call to grow more in love with Jesus. I heard that call as a young girl, and it has never left me. Through the years of serving the Lord, the call to love has only grown greater.

I pray that reading the Scriptures challenges you, just as they do me, and I am challenged to spread this message so that more may hear the invitation from the Lord: "Come."

If you agree that this message is important, I hope you will help distribute the book to others who may need to prayerfully consider what the Holy Spirit is saying; for the time is short, and now is our time to seek the Lord and His goodness and to draw closer to Him.

With love and blessings,

Barbara Lockhart

Prayer for Salvation

If you have never asked God to forgive you of your sins, if you have never asked Jesus to come into your heart, to change your life, and to be your Lord and Savior, please read these passages from the Bible and the prayer below.

For all have sinned; all fall short of God's glorious standard.

Romans 3:23

For God so loved the world that he gave his only Son, so that everyone who believes in him will not perish but have eternal life.

John 3:16

If we confess our sins to him, he is faithful and just to forgive us and to cleanse us from every wrong.

I John 1:9

Believe on the Lord Jesus and you will be saved....

Acts 16:31

Prayer

Lord God, I am sorry for every wrongdoing, for all my sins. I believe Jesus died and rose again for my salvation. I accept Jesus Christ as my Lord and Savior.

Jesus, I ask you to come into my heart. I give my life to live for you. Fill me with your love from this day on.

(Add whatever you want to say in your own words.)

Amen.

What's Next

Purchase or borrow from the library the New Testament of the Bible. Begin reading daily. Search out a good church where you can meet other Believers and share your new life in Christ. Pray daily, asking God to lead you and to fill you with His love and Holy Spirit.

Made in the USA
San Bernardino, CA
15 February 2018